PUERTO RICO
ITS OWN LAND

Written By: Elsie Guerrero
Illustrated By: Jasmine Mills
Formatted By: Jerome Vernell Jr.

ELSIE PUBLISHING CO.

WWW.ELSIEGUERRERO.COM

This story is dedicated to the children of Puerto Rico impacted by Hurricane Maria in 2017.

I want to acknowledge Margarita Varela-Rosa, Antonio Alejandro Camacho and the Inter-American University School of Law In Puerto Rico for inspiring this story.

Hola! My name is Luis and I am going to tell you a story about a beautiful island called Puerto Rico.

¡Hola! Mi nombre es Luis y voy a contarte una historia sobre una hermosa isla llamada Puerto Rico.

PUERTO RICO

ATLANTIC OCEAN

ISABELA

AGUADILLA

RINCÓN

ARECIBO

SAN JUAN

LAS MARIAS UTUADO BAYAMÓN

CERRO DE PUNTA

CAROLINA

EL YUNQUE

FAJARDO

ISLA DE CULEBRA

MAYAGÜEZ

CORDILLERA CENTRAL

CAGUAS

HUMACAO

SAN GERMÁN

ESPERANZA ISLA DE VIEQUES

BOSQUE ESTATAL DE GUANICA

PONCE

GUAYAMA

LAS MARIAS

PATILLAS

CARIBBEAN SEA

N

30 MI

30 KM

In the distance, between the Atlantic Ocean and the Caribbean Sea is the Island of Puerto Rico. The small island is beautiful and has awesome people and a diverse culture!

En la distancia, entre el Océano Atlántico y el Mar Caribe, se encuentra la isla de Puerto Rico. !La isla es pequeña pero hermosa, con gente jubilosa y una cultura diversa!

Puerto Rico was first inhabited by the indigenous people known as the Taino. The Tainos were one of the largest groups of inhabitants on the island.

La isla fue habitada primero por los indios Taínos. Los indios Taínos fueron uno de los pueblos indígenas más grandes de Puerto Rico.

In 1493, Christopher Columbus arrived on the island from Spain as part of an expansion mission paid for by the King and Queen of Spain to take over Puerto Rico.

En 1493, Cristóbal Colón llegó a la isla como parte de una misión de expansión financiada por la corona española para controlar Puerto Rico.

In 1897, local politicians persuaded the Spanish government to agree to an independent government. After many years of debate and tension, on July 17, 1898, Puerto Rico became an independent state, which meant they no longer were controlled by Spain.

En 1897, los políticos locales persuadieron al gobierno español para que aceptara un gobierno independiente. Después de mucha persuasión, el 17 de julio de 1898, Puerto Rico tuvo su primer gobierno autónomo y ya no mas fueron controlados por España.

Eight days later, the United States invaded Puerto Rico making it ones of their territories. This invasion took away the independence that many Puerto Ricans fought for.

Ocho días después, Estados Unidos invadió Puerto Rico convirtiéndolo en uno de sus territorios, lo que le quitó la autonomía por la que muchos puertorriqueños lucharon.

In 1901, the U.S. Supreme Court established the constitutional and political relationship between Puerto Rico and the United States. It gave Puerto Ricans no rights to vote for the president of the United States and no rights for the Puerto Rican representative in Congress to vote on laws.

En 1901, la Corte Suprema de los Estados Unidos estableció la relación constitucional y política entre Puerto Rico y los Estados Unidos. No otorgó a los puertorriqueños derechos para votar por el presidente de los Estados Unidos ni derechos para que el miembro del Congreso votara sobre la leyes federales.

In 1917, the United States congress passed the Jones Act. This gave Puerto Ricans U.S. citizenship, and remitted these new citizens to participate in World War I. It also gave Puerto Ricans the ability to travel to and from the United States freely.

En 1917, el Congreso de los Estados Unidos aprobó la Ley Jones que otorga a los puertorriqueños la ciudadanía estadounidense, lo que permitió a los puertorriqueños participar en la Primera Guerra Mundial y les permitió viajar a los Estados Unidos libremente.

IN 1947, the United States appointed its first Puerto Rican governor under the commonwealth, Jesus T. Piñero. He signed the Gag Law, which made it illegal to display the Puerto Rican flag, sing patriotic songs, speak about independence and fight for independence.

En 1947, los Estados Unidos nombraron al primer gobernador puertorriqueño, Jesús T. Piñero, quien firmó la Ley Gag que hizo ilegal exhibir la bandera puertorriqueña, cantar canciones patrióticas, hablar sobre la independencia y luchar por la independencia.

Congress would still legislate many aspects of Puerto Rico, such as citizenship, the way money is managed, foreign affairs and trade.

El Congreso todavía legislaría muchos aspectos de Puerto Rico, como la ciudadanía, la forma en que se maneja el dinero, los asuntos exteriores y el comercio.

Today, the strength of Puerto Rico culture remains consistent. A diverse formation of Taino, Spanish, and African culture is present throughout Puerto Rico.

Hoy en día, la fortaleza de la cultura de Puerto Rico sigue siendo consistente. Una diversa formación de cultura taína, española y africana está presente en todo Puerto Rico.

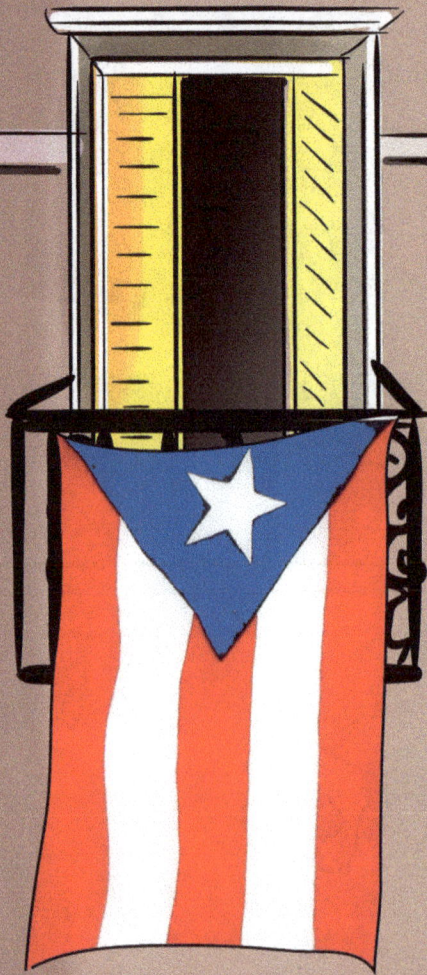

The Gag Law was removed in 1957 and Puerto Ricans began to display the flag every where. It became a key aspect of their culture.

Después de eliminar la prohibición de que no se les permitiera ondear la bandera, los puertorriqueños comenzaron a colocarla en todas partes. Se convirtió en parte esencial de su cultura.

The people of Puerto Rico are warm, welcoming and joyous. The richness of Puerto Rico's culture is seen by the beautiful blend of culture. At the center of many celebrations, lies music.

The music of Puerto Rico speaks of this history and culture. This can be heard in the traditional music of Bomba, Plena, and Salsa.

La gente de Puerto Rico es cálida, acogedora y alegre. La riqueza de la cultura de Puerto Rico es vista por la hermosa mezcla de cultura. En el centro de muchas celebraciones, se encuentra la música.

La música de Puerto Rico habla de esta historia y cultura. Esto se puede escuchar en la música tradicional de Bomba, Plena y Salsa.

Many modern popular singers originated from Puerto Rico. Influenced by hip hop, Latin American and Caribbean music, Reggaetón, has risen to be a popular music in today's pop culture, which originated from Puerto Rico.

Muchos cantantes populares modernos son puertorriqueños. El reggaetón, se ha convertido en una música popular en la cultura pop actual, y se originó en Puerto Rico.

Puerto Rico's most popular dish is Mofongo, made with fried plantains, salt garlic and oil in a wooden pilon. Another popular dish is arroz con gandules, a combination of rice, pigeon peas and pork, cooked in the same pot with sofrito.

Uno de los platos más populares de Puerto Rico es el mofongo, hecho con plátanos fritos, ajo salado y aceite en un pilón de madera. Otro plato popular es el arroz con gándules, una combinación de arroz, frijoles y cerdo, que se cocina en la misma olla con sofrito.

Puerto Rico is surrounded by many beaches because it is an island, which makes it different and unique from Spain and the United States.

Puerto Rico está rodeado de muchas playas, lo que lo hace diferente y único de España y Estados Unidos.

The majority of Puerto Ricans practice the Roman Catholic religion under the spiritual leadership of a Pope. The island's cathedral church in San Juan is visited by hundreds of people every day for prayer and worship.

La mayoría de los puertorriqueños se consideran católicos romanos bajo el liderazgo espiritual del Papa. Cientos de personas visitan La Catedral de San Juan todos los días para orar.

Puerto Rico has a popular tropical rainforest where it rains year round called the Caribbean National. But in 2007, United States President George W. Bush, changed the name to El Yunque to reflect the cultural and historical feelings of the Puerto Rican people.

Puerto Rico tiene un popular bosque tropical donde llueve todo el año llamado Caribbean National. Pero en 2007, el presidente de los Estados Unidos, George W. Bush, cambió el nombre a El Yunque para reflejar los sentimientos culturales e históricos del los puertorriqueños.

EL YUNQUE
NATIONAL
FOREST

U.S DEPT OF AGRICULTURE

Puerto Rico is a beautiful island,
with its own distinctive identity.
Puerto Rico is its own land.

Viva Puerto Rico Libre!

Puerto Rico es una isla hermosa, con su identidad distintiva. Puerto Rico es su propia tierra.

!Viva Puerto Rico Libre!

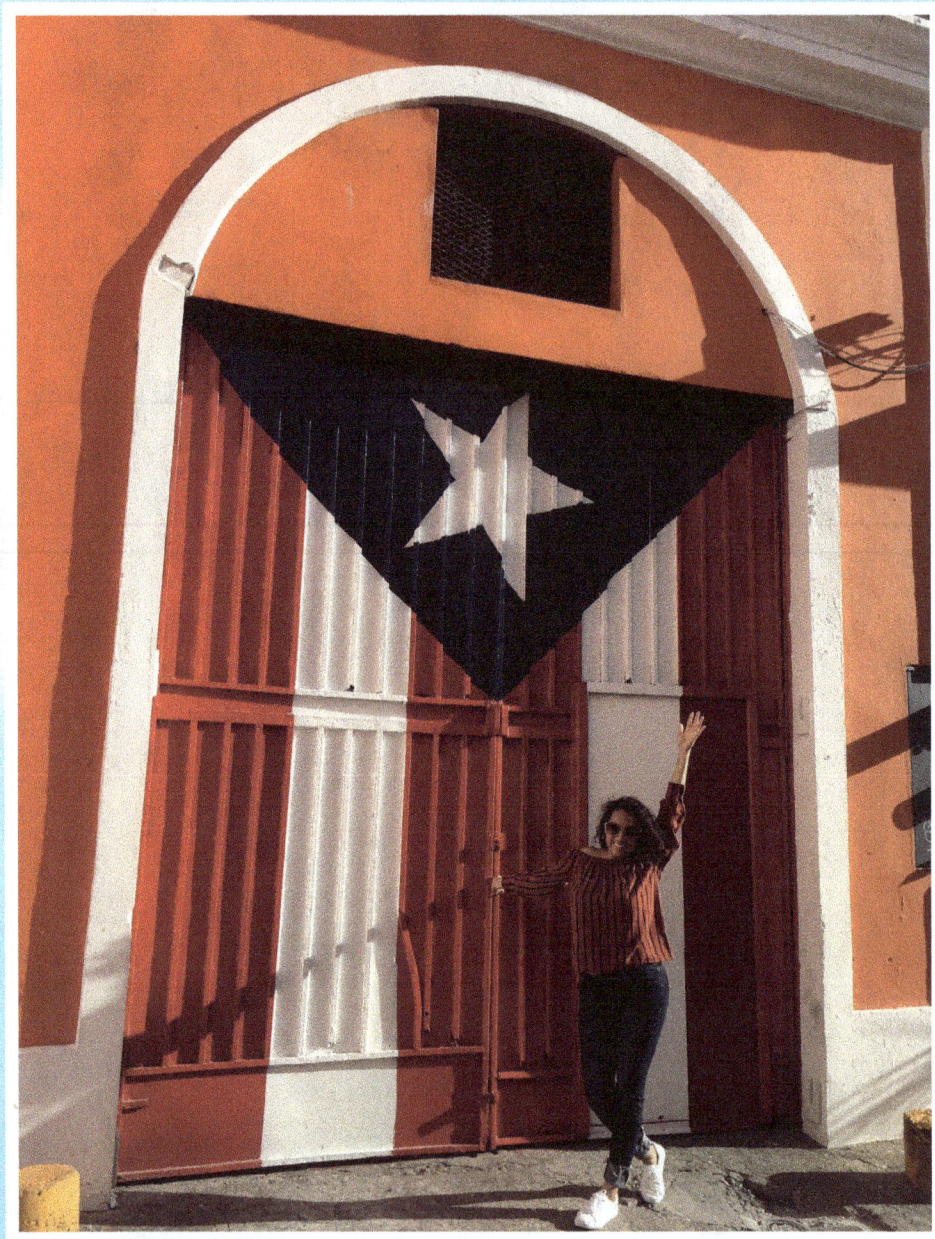

Elsie Guerrero is the author of A New Life in America and Bringing Back History: The Untold Story of the Unlawful Mexican Repatriation. She was inspired to write children's books by children who shared their stories with her. Puerto Rico, Its Own Land was inspired by her trip to Puerto Rico where she learned about the legal and political issues surrounding Puerto Rico. She wanted to share how beautiful Puerto Rico was and the contribution the island brings to the world.

Like Puerto Rico, Its Own Land? Check out other books written by Elsie Guerrero.

¿Te gustó Puerto Rico, Su Propia Tierra ? Echa un vistazo a otros libros escritos por Elsie Guerrero.

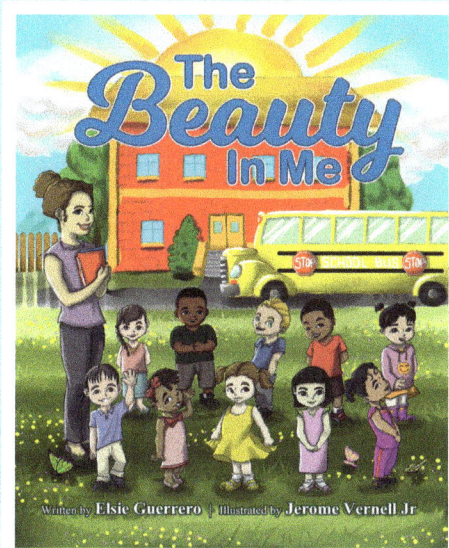

The Beauty In Me
Written by Elsie Guerrero | Illustrated by Jerome Vernell Jr

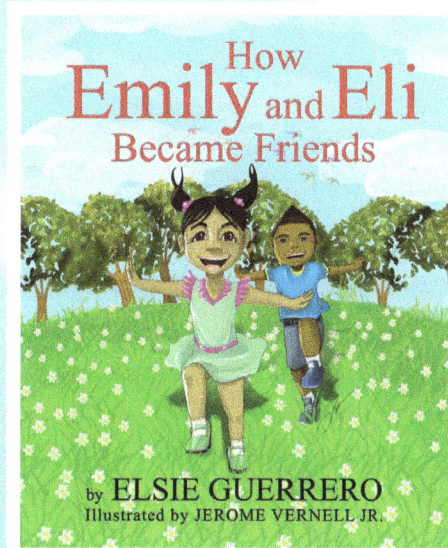

How Emily and Eli Became Friends
by ELSIE GUERRERO
Illustrated by JEROME VERNELL JR.

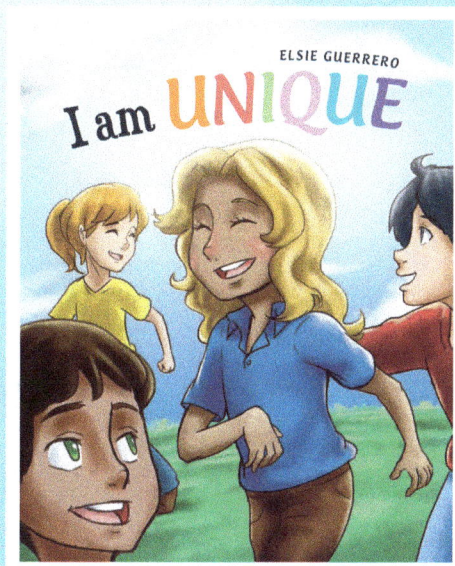

ELSIE GUERRERO
I am UNIQUE

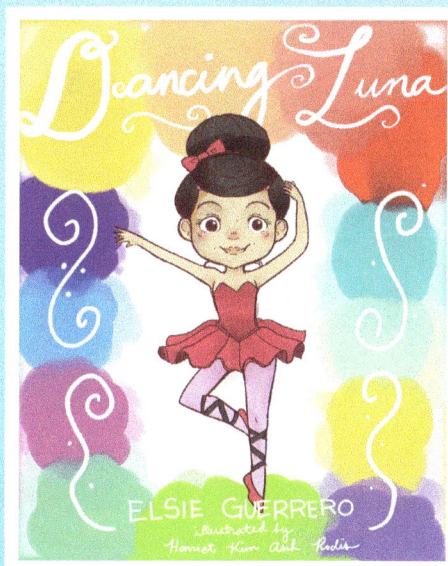

Dancing Luna
ELSIE GUERRERO
illustrated by
Harriet Kim Anh Rodis

www.ELSIEGUERRERO.com

Spread Awareness. Promote Inclusion.
Difunde conciencia. Promueve inclusión.

www.ingramcontent.com/pod-product-compliance
Lightning Source LLC
Chambersburg PA
CBHW062012090426
42811CB00005B/833